A PORTRAIT
OF THE ARTIST
AS A YOUNG MAN

F 16

(2)

NOTES

Including
Chapter Summaries and Commentaries
Glossary of Persons, Places and Terms
Questions for Review

By
Katherine A. Lilly, M.A.
University of Nebraska

Cliff's Notes
INCORPORATED
LINCOLN, NEBRASKA   68501

CONTENTS

1547673

INTRODUCTION

James Joyce wrote only six books—a slim volume of verse, a play, and four books of fiction—and yet he is acknowledged as the greatest literary craftsman of our time. A summary, such as this, of his techniques and themes is a helpful supplement to an understanding of his writing, but it can in no way communicate the humanity, the humor, and the virtuosity of his genius. Joyce should be read and reread for an appreciation of what he is doing. The content of his writing seems inexhaustible. He spent well over ten years writing each of his books, and he suggested that his readers would do well to spend the same amount of time in reading them.

Joyce's work as a whole is difficult to place in a literary pigeon-hole. In his early work we can see the influence of the literary schools of naturalism and psychological realism. But ultimately, he became a transitional figure not connected with a particular literary genre or movement. When he left Ireland as a young man, he cut himself away from the Irish literary renaissance going on at the time and became, in fact, a school by himself.

Dubliners (1914), a book of short stories, is written in relatively clear, understandable prose. In *A Portrait of the Artist As a Young Man* (1916) he was beginning to experiment with more complex techniques and multiple levels of meaning. By the time we reach *Ulysses* (1922), his major contribution to literature, his writing is heavily weighted with symbolic and mythic content. His final work, *Finnegans Wake* (1939), is so dense and experimental as to be almost incomprehensible to the average reader, but its richness does yield to diligent digging by the patient student of Joyce.

All of Joyce's books of fiction are closely related thematically. Many of the same characters and situations appear in each book. It would seem almost essential to be familiar with *A Portrait of the Artist As a Young Man* before tackling *Ulysses*. The structure of *Ulysses* is based on Homer's *Odyssey,* and the first three sections of *Ulysses,* the so-called Telemachia, are devoted almost exclusively to Stephen Dedalus, the hero of *Portrait of the Artist* (hereafter we shall frequently use this shortened form of the title).

The final chapter of *Portrait of the Artist* is hard going indeed if we do not understand that Joyce was preparing a bridge into *Ulysses*. The audacious, eccentric Stephen of *Ulysses* whose complex mind is absorbed in Middle English texts is rooted in *Portrait of the Artist*. And if Stephen seems insufferable and humorless in his interminable conversations in Chapter V, it is because the tragic effect of *Ulysses* is dependent upon this character development.

This novel is one of the most convincing portraits of a young man ever to be written. But the reader must remember that Stephen is an exceptional child, bookish and introspective. At an early age he senses his superiority to his environment, his companions, and the members of his family. And yet, as H. G. Wells observed, one believes in Stephen Dedalus as one believes in few characters in fiction.

IS STEPHEN DEDALUS JAMES JOYCE?

A Portrait of the Artist As a Young Man is based on the first twenty years of James Joyce's life, but the true relationship, biographically, between Joyce and Stephen Dedalus remains a disputed question. Scholars continue to disagree on the extent to which Joyce was committed to Stephen's viewpoint.

Some critics view this novel as an uncompromisingly truthful portrait of Joyce's earlier self, written with astonishing objectivity and detachment. Others consider the book a satire on the alienated artist. It is likely that Joyce was attempting to depict in the character of Stephen Dedalus the image of the universal artist complete with many of the stereotypes we associate with the artist-type. And one of the most popular stereotypes of the artist is social alienation. Thus, we see embodied in Stephen the conflict of the artist versus society.

But, for the most part, we may consider this novel a fictionalized autobiography in which Joyce indulged in frequent distortions of fact in order to further his aesthetic purposes. Joyce's associates contend that he was a much more well-rounded and well-adjusted person than Stephen Dedalus but the author himself reminded his readers that this is, after all, a portrait of a *young man,* possessing many of the defects of youth.

Stephen Dedalus, as the young Joyce, is endowed with the same delicate physique, weak eyesight, and subtle intelligence of the author; Joyce even signed some of his early stories "Stephen Daedalus." Therefore, biographical knowledge is a useful tool for an understanding of Joyce's writing.

LIFE AND BACKGROUND

Joyce was born in 1882 in a Dublin suburb, the eldest son of fifteen children, only ten of whom survived infancy. Moderately well-to-do, his family sent him to a Jesuit boy's boarding school, Clongowes Wood College, at the age of six. He remained there, returning home only for holidays, until he was nine years old. At that time the family fortunes began to decline, and it was financially impossible to send Joyce back to Clongowes. Two years later, through the efforts of his father, he was enrolled in another Jesuit school, Belvedere College, where he studied until he was sixteen. At Belvedere the brilliance of his mind became evident, but it was a mind constricted by convention and thwarted by poverty. The shabbiness of life around him stung the young genius and filled him with a sense of futility.

Joyce entered University College, Dublin, in 1899 at the age of seventeen. During these decisive years (re-created in Chapter V of *Portrait of the Artist*) the rebellious young spirit resolved to sever his ties with family, church, and country and devote his life to creative art. Receiving his degree at the age of twenty, Joyce prepared to leave Ireland, and this is as far as *Portrait of the Artist* takes us.

Joyce did in fact go to Paris where he began in 1904 to work on *A Portrait of the Artist As a Young Man,* rewriting and revising it over a ten year period. It was first published in England in serial form between 1914-1915. He returned briefly to Ireland when his mother died and met Nora Barnacle who returned to the continent with him and settled in Trieste, Italy. Opposed to marriage, they lived together for twenty-seven years and raised two children before they were legally married, "for testamentary reasons."

His professional career was marked by continual struggles to get his work published. In 1912 he made his last trip to Ireland in an unsuccessful effort to get his book of short stories, *Dubliners,* in print. But the publishers feared the frankness of the book and refused to do the job. It was finally published in England in 1914. *Ulysses* was published in Paris in 1922, but it was not until 1933 when Judge John M. Woolsey issued his famous decision, ruling that it was not pornographic, that the book could be published in the United States. His final work, *Finnegans Wake,* which was seventeen years in the writing, was published in 1939. Two years later Joyce died of a perforated ulcer in Zurich, Switzerland, at the age of fifty-nine.

Above all, Joyce was an innovator; the revolutionary literary techniques that he introduced in *Ulysses* signalled the beginning of a new kind of writing, the traditional form and methods having been completed or exhausted in this "novel to end all novels."[1]

In rewriting and revising *Portrait of the Artist,* the nearly one thousand page original manuscript was considerably foreshortened and certain logical connections in the narrative were eliminated. The reader must supply these for himself. In remolding his own past, Joyce achieved an extraordinarily sharp, objective, and tightly economical book. Every word counts.

The author's attitude toward Stephen is amused, detached, and sympathetic. What we have here is a mind contemplating itself and re-creating its own development. Joyce shares with Stephen a personal philosophy of passivity in action, energy in thought, and tenacity in conviction.

Joyce's brooding sensibility resulted in an attitude toward society which was often caustic and contemptuous. Critics have

---

[1]Harry Levin, *James Joyce* (Norfolk, Conn.: 1960), p. 207.

pointed out that *Portrait of the Artist* is not only an indictment of his background but an attempt at self-justification. The incidents recounted of his childhood are uniformly unhappy, each event marred by the insensitivity of others. The precocious, often arrogant Stephen Dedalus is unable to cope with real people in real life situations; he is a hero only in the wanderings of his own imagination. In this highly personal novel we see that although Joyce's genius was universal in scope, his approach to writing is perhaps the most self-centered in English literature.

STYLE AND LITERARY TECHNIQUES

Joyce's writing is an elaborate structure of analogies, correspondences, and verbal associations. The actions of his characters are revealed by indirection, introspection, and evasion. The plot of *Portrait of the Artist* is unfolded by means of meditations and soliloquies. Instead of straightforward description, we often have the quality of incantation. This is especially evident at the end of Chapter IV, the climax of the novel, where the writing can best be described as "word painting."

It is generally accepted that Joyce's near blindness had an effect on his writing which is marked by auditory rather than visual images. Joyce was an accomplished listener; his keen ear for the sounds of words and his unusual sensitivity to the language has never been surpassed. Light images are important to his literary technique; they often have the luminous shine-through quality of stained glass. Notice this technique in Stephen's description of roses in the opening pages of the novel. The reader will also observe that the most striking images are those of coldness, dampness, and whiteness.

Joyce introduced at least three new literary techniques: the stream-of-consciousness, the epiphany, and the use of myth.

THE STREAM-OF-CONSCIOUSNESS TECHNIQUE

The advances of modern psychology have been a great shaping force in the literature of the twentieth century. The drama of the mind of the individual becomes the writer's focus of interest.

The term "stream-of-consciousness" is borrowed from modern psychoanalysis and describes the "free association" of ideas in the human mind. Just as floating objects are carried along somewhat haphazardly by the current of a stream or river, so do thoughts and images travel through our minds in an apparently unorganized, illogical succession.

James Joyce and Virginia Woolf were the first writers to transfer this mental phenomenon to English literature and exploit it as a literary technique. Instead of simply stating what the character is thinking, the author writes as though he were inside the mind of the character. The result is an "interior monologue" or "direct quotation of the mind."

The "action" takes place and the plot develops through the mind of the characters. The adventures of Stephen Dedalus are of an emotional and intellectual nature. The real struggles take place in his mind, and so, thought becomes "action." What he does and sees is not so significant as what he *thinks* as he is doing and seeing. The actual conflicts are not usually dramatized. An external event or situation along with all the associations and recollections which it arouses in Stephen's mind are presented more or less simultaneously.

In this connection it should be noted that there is an uncommon amount of walking done in *Portrait of the Artist*. It is the principal "action" of the story.

Stephen says at the end of *Portrait of the Artist:* "The past is consumed in the present and the present is living only because it brings forth the future." Joyce was ever concerned with the past's impingement on the present. One cannot escape the past; it determines the present. Other twentieth-century writers have developed this theme, notably William Faulkner. Stephen Dedalus has a sense of history and though he says, "I am not responsible for the past," he sees the consequences of the past all around him in the present. This merging of past and present in Joyce's writing is expressed by means of the stream-of-consciousness technique.

THE EPIPHANY

In Joyce's writing, an epiphany is a sudden spiritual revelation or manifestion which the character experiences usually at a moment of crisis. It is as if a veil is lifted and one is able to see the essential quality or unity of some idea, event, or person. Such a spiritual breakthrough could be triggered by something as insignificant as a sound or a gesture.

Stephen's major epiphany occurs at the end of Chapter IV as he stands on the seashore gazing at an unknown girl. Stephen suddenly sees himself clearly for the first time and he knows what he must do. There is no turning back after this point.

THE USE OF MYTH

Joyce was seeking a means of organization or pattern to structure his work and, being thoroughly acquainted with the body of western and eastern mythology, he employed it very consciously wherever he could. He was interested in the aesthetic relevance of myth, the universal truths or meanings which the myths embodied. He drew from these ancient and timeless stories and manipulated them to suit his own aesthetic purposes in order to deepen the dimensions of his characters and to say something about modern man. T. S. Eliot, for one, attached enormous significance to Joyce's mythical method. It was, he said, "a step toward making the modern world possible in art."

Although the mythic content of this book is relatively thin when compared to *Ulysses* or *Finnegans Wake,* still one may discover the foundations of the technique in this novel. Stephen's last name, Dedalus, is the wedge whereby myth and symbol enter the story. Joyce used the myth of Daedalus and Icarus as a kind of backdrop for *Portrait of the Artist.*

The Myth of Daedalus and Icarus

Daedalus, we recall, was the gifted architect of ancient Crete who was commissioned by King Minos to design a labyrinth as a place of confinement for the monster Minotaur. Daedalus contrived a labyrinth so intricate that escape from it was virtually impossible. But falling into disfavor with the king, Daedalus himself, along with his son, Icarus, were eventually imprisoned there.

Not to be outdone, the "famous artificer," Daedalus, explained to his son, Icarus, that although their escape was checked by land and sea, the open sky was free. He devised two pairs of wings, and father and son immediately took flight from Crete.

Daedalus warned his impetuous son not to fly too high lest the heat of the sun melt the glue and his wings fall off. But Icarus, filled with a sense of power in his flight, disregarded his father's commands and soon his wings, heated by the sun, fell off, and he plunged into the sea, the waters closing over him.

In Joyce's symbolic language Dublin is a modern labyrinth, a place of confinement, from which Stephen must escape. For Stephen, the city represents a shabby, dusty world of restraint and spiritual paralysis.

At times Stephen is identified with the crafty inventor, Daedalus (his namesake), and at other times with Icarus, the ill-fated rebellious son.

By juxtaposing Stephen with the ancient hero of myth, comparisons with past and present can be drawn.

GENERAL PLOT SUMMARY AND STRUCTURE

Portrait of the Artist As a Young Man is a novel of development in which we follow a young boy's initiation into the adult world. The theme of the novel is growth or the formation of character.

The novel moves from a highly impersonal opening section to the intimate, personal entries in Stephen's diary at the end. Psychologically, there is a movement from a state of indecision on Stephen's part to some degree of certitude in the concluding section.

The structure of the book (five chapters) can be compared to the structure of a classical drama. The turning point or climax occurs at the end of the fourth chapter, followed by the denouement or working out of the resolution in the fifth chapter.

CHAPTER I

The opening chapter covers the period of Stephen's childhood from approximately age six to nine years. He is enrolled at a Jesuit boy's boarding school, Clongowes Wood College, returning home only for holidays.

Joyce recounts three or four incidents which are significant in this period of Stephen's life: Stephen is confined to the school infirmary with a fever, having been pushed in a ditch of water by a thoughtless classmate; Stephen has Christmas dinner with his family and a heated political argument ensues; and, finally, Stephen is punished unjustly by the prefect of studies; whereupon he goes to the rector of the school to explain that he was excused from study because his glasses were broken by another rude classmate.

CHAPTER II

Stephen is now attending another Jesuit boys' school, Belvedere College. Chapters II, III, and IV cover the period of Stephen's life from about age eleven to sixteen. We see the awakening of religious doubts and a growing absorption in the world of books.

The incidents recounted become more disconnected and less clearly defined. Stephen participates in a school play, accompanies his father on a trip to Cork, and wins an essay contest. His personal frustrations and growing sexual instincts lead to his first sexual experience in the brothel district of Dublin. This section is the first of three undramatic climaxes in the novel.

CHAPTER III

Stephen attends a three day spiritual retreat at Belvedere College. The priest's eloquent sermons move Stephen to reform and, after confessing his sins to a priest, he resolves to begin a new life of sanctity. This retreat forms the ethical center of the novel.

CHAPTER IV

Stephen's impressive piety prompts the head of the school to ask him if he would like to be a priest. Stephen's soul-struggles continue along with a mounting dissatisfaction with his life. Finally, he experiences a spiritual breakthrough, his "epiphany," at the end of the chapter. This is the second undramatic climax and the turning point of the action.

CHAPTER V

Stephen is now enrolled at University College, Dublin. The final chapter covers the period of Stephen's life from age seventeen to twenty.

Stephen's aesthetic philosophy is set forth by means of his conversations with the Dean of Studies, and classmates Cranly and Lynch.

Stephen resolves to make a final break with the Catholic Church, his family, and his country, and dedicate his life to creative art. The book ends on the verge of Stephen's exile which is the final undramatic climax of the novel.

Note to the Reader: *Throughout the general narrative of* Portrait of the Artist, *Joyce mainly used the past tense; in dialogue, he mainly uses the present tense. Because of the nature of summary and commentary, however, we have not always been able to preserve Joyce's verb usage in this outline.*

CAST OF CHARACTERS

Stephen Dedalus is the only major character in this novel, which is almost exclusively *his* story. The other characters are significant only to the extent that Stephen allows them to affect his life and occupy his thoughts. Other than Stephen, his father, Simon Dedalus, and his friend, Cranly, are perhaps the most significant minor characters. Many of the characters listed below are only vaguely sketched and some appear in only one or two brief scenes.

A. *The Dedalus Family*
1. Stephen Dedalus — the son and hero of the novel.

2. Simon Dedalus — Stephen's father.

3. May Dedalus — Stephen's mother.

4. Maurice Dedalus — Stephen's younger brother.

5. Uncle Charles — a relative who lives with the family until his death.

6. Aunt Dante (Mrs. Riordan) — her most important part in the novel is at the Christmas dinner in Chapter I.

7. Katey, Maggy, and Boody — Stephen's sisters referred to vaguely in Chapter V.

B. *Characters Close to the Dedalus Family*
1. Mr. Casey (John) — he attends the family Christmas dinner in Chapter I and is active in the political argument by defending the dead Irish leader, Charles Stewart Parnell.

2. Eileen Vance — Stephen's childhood sweetheart. Later in the novel Stephen refers to an "Emma," and writes poetry to "E— —C— —," but the three females are never clearly distinguished from each other.

C. Clongowes Wood College (Chapter I)

Stephen's teachers or masters:

1. Father Arnall—the Latin teacher who later appears as the retreat master in Chapter III.

2. Father Dolan—the prefect of studies who punishes Stephen in Latin class with a pandybat.

3. Father Conmee—the rector whom Stephen goes to see in the castle.

4. Brother Michael—he takes care of Stephen while he is sick in the infirmary.

5. Mr. Gleeson, Mr. Barrett (Paddy), and Mr. Harford—all teachers referred to briefly.

Stephen's classmates:

1. Fleming—he is punished also by Father Dolan in Latin class.

2. Jack Lawton—he is head of the Lancaster team which competes with Stephen's team, the Yorkists, in class contests.

3. Nasty Roche—he is important because he questions Stephen about his family and his odd last name.

4. Wells—the rough student who pushes Stephen in the ditch of dirty water and causes him to become ill.

5. Athy—Stephen's companion in the infirmary; his father is a race horse owner.

Other students mentioned briefly: Rody Kickham, Cecil Thunder, Simon Moonan, Hamilton Rowan, Dominic Kelly, Tusker Boyle, Jimmy Magee, Paddy Rath, Corrigan, Cantwell, Saurin.

1. Aubrey Mills—Stephen's summer companion at Blackrock before he enters Belvedere College.

2. Mike Flynn — Stephen's track trainer during the summer at Blackrock.

D. Belvedere College (Chapters II-III-IV)
1. Vincent Heron — classmate who shares the leadership of the school with Stephen.

2. Wallis — Vincent Heron's friend who appears the night of the school play.

3. Bertie Tallon — a boy who takes part in the play.

4. Boland — a classmate whom Stephen calls "a dunce."

5. Nash — a classmate whom Stephen calls "an idler."

6. Father Arnall — the Jesuit priest who conducts the three-day retreat which Stephen attends.

7. Mr. Tate — the English master.

8. Johnny Cashman — an old cronie of Simon Dedalus' whom they meet on a trip to Cork.

E. University College, Dublin (Chapter V)
1. Dean of Studies — an English Jesuit priest with whom Stephen discusses philosophy.

2. Cranly — Stephen's closest friend and confidant.

3. Lynch — a student who takes long walks with Stephen during which Stephen explains his aesthetic philosophy.

4. Davin — the "peasant student" and ardent Irish nationalist.

5. McCann — the student who is heading the signing of the petition for social equality and world peace.

6. Temple — the "gypsy student" who admires Stephen's knowledge and hates Cranly.

Other students briefly mentioned: Moynihan, MacAlister, Donovan, Dixon, O'Keefe, Goggins, Glynn, Shuley, Ennis, Connelly.

CHAPTER I

Summary

As the novel opens, the reader is placed somewhat abruptly in the mind of a very small boy. The disconnected, fragmentary prose captures the primary impact of the sights and sounds of life. This is the coming to consciousness of the individual, in particular, Stephen Dedalus, the hero of *Portrait of the Artist*.

Coldness, wetness, warmth, color, animal noises, and smells, all merge in his memory to form the first impressions of his life. A few incidents are flashed briefly before us — Stephen walks down a country lane and sees a "moo-cow"; then Stephen wets his bed and remembers his mother singing a song for him. He is beginning to order and evaluate the fragments of his first experience of life.

The Dedalus family is introduced — Stephen's father, Simon Dedalus, and his mother, May Dedalus, and the relatives, Uncle Charles and Mrs. Riordan (Dante). Eileen Vance, the little girl Stephen plans to marry someday, is mentioned.

We move immediately to Stephen's first school experience, the boys' boarding school known as Clongowes Wood College (equivalent to a grade and prep school). We follow by way of Stephen's thoughts the incidents which Joyce selected because of their enormous significance in the shaping of this sensitive boy.

The progression of events is rather scrambled and disconnected. Stephen's farewells to his family on the first day of school are described, along with a ball game on the playing field, study hall, and evening prayers.

Stephen catches a cold as a result of being pushed into a ditch of dirty water. Wells, a rough and boisterous classmate, was the rude offender. Stephen is put under the care of Brother Michael in the infirmary. There he meets Athy, the son of a racehorse owner. Frightened and ill, Stephen's depression deepens. He begins to imagine that he is about to die. But he is comforted by the thought that the wrongdoer, Wells, would then be filled with remorse for bringing about the untimely death of Stephen Dedalus.

Stephen's mind, semi-delirious, wanders to other grisly thoughts. He recalls the story some of the old servants told of the ghost of a marshal in a white cloak which appeared in the castle, the old building where the priests live.

The next scene is Christmas dinner at home with Stephen's parents, Uncle Charles, Dante, and the guest, Mr. Casey (John). Inevitably, an argument on politics develops and succeeds in ruining the holiday dinner despite Mrs. Dedalus' efforts to quiet tempers.

Charles Stewart Parnell, an Irish political leader who had recently died, was the controversial subject of the argument. Mr. Casey, a loyal supporter of Parnell, who was jailed for giving political speeches on the subject, agrees with Uncle Charles and Simon Dedalus that Parnell was deeply wronged by the Irish people, the worst offender being the Catholic Church. Parnell's personal morals were the basis of the dispute. When the powerful leader took as his mistress, Kitty O'Shea, the Church denounced him from the pulpit as an adulterer. The men at the table criticize the Church for getting involved in politics while Mrs. Riordan fiercely defends the Church as guardian of public morality. Enraged, she marches out of the room slamming the door behind her while Mr. Casey and Simon, their fury spent, bow their heads and sob quietly for their betrayed hero.

The next scene is back at Clongowes. Stephen, always the outsider, listens to a group of classmates discussing the fate of the boys who have stolen and consumed altar wine from the sacristy. The question is whether they will be flogged or expelled.

Eileen comes into his thoughts again. Stephen remembers a fleeting incident in which she put her ivory white hands in his pocket as they were playing together. She is associated in his mind with the Blessed Virgin, and phrases from a litany — "Tower of Ivory," "House of Gold" — are intoned to make this association explicit.

Stephen sits in Father Arnall's Latin class during the course of which the prefect of studies, Father Dolan, enters wielding a pandybat intending to beat the hands of any "lazy idle schemers." Stephen watches in terror as he disciplines one of his classmates, Fleming. Father Dolan notices that Stephen is not doing his lessons with the other boys. The trembling boy explains that his glasses were broken, and he was thus excused from his studies. The powerful priest scoffs at this excuse and orders Stephen to put out his hands for punishment. Humiliated beyond words, tears of indignation burn on Stephen's cheeks as he is punished.

With the encouragement of his classmates, Stephen's sense of injustice grows and he resolves to report the incident to the rector. After dinner he makes the long and painful journey to "the castle" where the priests live and manages to tell the rector that his glasses were knocked off by a cyclist and that he has written home for new ones. The momentousness of the event in Stephen's mind is undercut by the casual attitude of the rector, Father Conmee, who rights the matter with some brief words of sympathy and promptly dismisses a somewhat comforted Stephen.

Commentary

Certain thematic motifs help to unify this novel. In literature, a motif is a repeated idea or image which creates a thematic pattern. Like a figure in a carpet it affects the entire design, depending on how often and where it is repeated. It not only enriches the content of the work, but it aids the reader in determining the major ideas that the novel is concerned with.

In Joyce's writing, motifs usually have symbolic significance. Certain words or images may suggest an abstract idea or an unconscious need or desire of a particular character. An example of this kind of motif is what we will refer to as the *blindness motif,* although it could be described by other names as well.

Early in the novel we should notice Stephen's preoccupation with light and darkness, vision and blindness. To mention only a few instances of this pattern we see it in the childhood verse that runs through Stephen's mind: "Pull out his eyes/ Apologize...." And later on it is evident when Stephen contemplates fearfully: "But, O, the road there between the trees was dark! You would be lost in the dark."

This so-called *blindness motif* serves to emphasize the plight of a sensitive young boy who is searching for many things. For one, he is seeking insight into the adult world that he sees around him.

The *mythic motif* also begins early in the novel. Stephen is puzzled when his classmate, Nasty Roche, says to him: "What kind of name is that?" Stephen's unusual last name, Dedalus, grows in significance for him and the reader when considered in the light of the myth of Daedalus and Icarus. Later in the novel Stephen makes specific references to this myth and identifies himself with it directly. Joyce frequently uses images of birds or flight or water to develop this motif.

The argument that disrupts Christmas dinner in the Dedalus household should be understood in the light of the political situation at the time. The fall of Charles Stewart Parnell was a deeply felt political upheaval in Ireland. It engendered feelings of bitterness and betrayal, and this mood is reflected throughout *Portrait of the Artist.*

We should also notice in this first chapter how Stephen's alienation from others, his uniqueness, develops. He is continually on the periphery of his companions' conversations, listening attentively but comprehending only vaguely what they mean. The contrast between his companions and himself is very marked — they are rough and earthy; he is sensitive and spiritual.

CHAPTER II

Summary

It is summer, and Stephen is home from school with his family. The chapter opens with a brief vignette of Uncle Charles, sitting in the outhouse smoking his pipe.

Stephen builds up his delicate physique running around a track in the park, his athletic endeavors being supervised by Uncle Charles and a trainer, Mike Flynn. He spends many hours walking in the country around Dublin with his father and his uncle.

But, more and more, he retreats to the world of books. *The Count of Monte Cristo* satisfies his boyish hunger for adventure and romance, but he also acts out this hunger in nightly forays and battles with a friend, Aubrey Mills.

Stephen does not return to Clongowes, and he is vaguely aware that his father's financial reverses are the reason why he cannot go back to school. The gradual changes in the household as a result of dwindling finances undermine his security and are so many slight shocks to his sensitive personality. He amuses himself riding about the neighborhood on the milk carts. As his imagination continues to develop, he slips into frequent romantic reveries about an ideal female. Sometimes he refers to her as Eileen, sometimes the fictional Mercedes, sometimes Emma, or simply "E– –C– –," and sometimes she remains undefined. He longs for the moment when he will shed his boyhood and become a man.

The Dedalus family moves from Blackrock, a suburb of Dublin, to a less fashionable (and respectable) neighborhood in the city – the first of many moves which occur as the family fortunes decline. Uncle Charles is becoming senile. The cheerless house, the complexity of the city, and Stephen's mounting restlessness, cause him to withdraw deeper into a dream-like world of unreality. He escapes what he considers the squalor and insincerity of his life by becoming more and more detached from it spiritually.

Incidents become less defined and more impressionistic. He is sitting in the kitchen of his aunt's house...he is in a room with an old woman, and a girl comes in named Ellen...he is at a children's party, observing it in gloomy detachment. "She" (the undefined female) appears again at the party and her eyes taunt him. He has an encounter with her on a tram ride, and he contemplates kissing her but remains in anguished silence as she alights from the tram leaving him alone. His quarters at home are a "bare upper room"—indicative of the poverty that has overtaken the Dedalus family. Here the solitary adolescent tries to compose Byronic love poems to E— —C— —.

Simon Dedalus uses what influence he has left to get his two sons, Stephen and a younger brother, Maurice, into Belvedere College, a prep school run by Jesuit priests.

In the next scene Stephen participates in a school play at Belvedere. Two years after the children's party, Stephen's precocious personality has developed considerably. He has acquired an urbane sophistication, and his feelings of superiority are evident in his condescending attitude toward his classmates. Waiting to go on stage, Stephen stands outside in the dark and talks with two boys, Vincent Heron and Wallis. Heron and Stephen are the uncontested leaders of the school. The loud bantering and "mirthless laughter" of Heron and Wallis irritate Stephen—

> His sensitive nature was still smarting under the lashes of an undivined and squalid way of life. His soul was still disquieted and cast down by the dull phenomenon of Dublin.

His companions ride Stephen about his relationship with a girl, and they press him to admit it. Finally, he satisfies their desire for a crude retort by reciting in mock seriousness the *Confiteor* of the Mass.

There is a weekly essay contest at Belvedere which Stephen generally wins. One week Mr. Tate, the English master, accuses Stephen of writing heresy in his essay concerning the Creator and the soul.

A few nights after this public chiding, he is stopped while walking along the road by three classmates, including Heron. They take pleasure in baiting and provoking Stephen to anger. Stephen senses their mockery when they ask him to state who he thinks is the greatest poet and the greatest prose writer. The other two boys are Boland, whom Stephen considers the dunce of the class, and Nash, who is an idler. Stephen answers that Cardinal Newman has the best prose style and that Byron is the greatest poet. They retort that Byron was a heretic and immoral; Stephen replies that they know nothing about the subject. They begin to beat Stephen with a cane to get him to admit that Byron was no good, shouting in his ears, "Here, catch hold of this heretic." Finally, his tormentors tear off laughing wildly and leaving the enraged Stephen standing in the dark, blinded with tears.

We return briefly to the night of the school play. The girl his companions referred to comes into his thoughts again. Preparing to go on stage, Stephen muses on the insincerity of his friends and considers it a "sorry anticipation of manhood." He feels a growing disillusionment with the adult world that surrounds him. The girl who has occupied his thoughts is sitting in the audience, and he dreads the thought of her watching him acting out his humiliating role, that of a farcical pedagogue. Immediately after the play, he rushes out of the theater, brushing past his family, and runs off into the night by himself filled with "wounded pride and fallen hope and baffled desire."

Stephen and his father, Simon, go by train to visit the city of Cork. The purpose of the trip is to sell his father's property at auction and also to familiarize Stephen with all the old haunts of Simon Dedalus' boyhood. Stephen is, of course, totally disinterested. During the train ride Stephen's father begins a nostalgic evocation of old times and old friends dead and gone. His mood is encouraged by frequent gulps from his pocket flask. Stephen remains utterly detached and listens "without sympathy." We are told that Uncle Charles has died. His father finally drops off to sleep as Stephen gazes broodingly at the passing countryside.

In their room at the Victoria Hotel in Cork, Simon Dedalus' vanity and exaggerated self-esteem become evident as he preens before a mirror "twirling the points of his moustache." They eat breakfast and set out for the father's *alma mater*, Queens College.

Simon and the old porter at the college lead a bored and restless Stephen around the campus. With mounting irritation Stephen listens to the stories he has heard a hundred times and "the names of the scattered and dead revellers who had been the companions of his father's youth." They enter the anatomy theater (lecture Hall), and the boy is struck by the word "foetus" which has been carved on one of the desks. It evokes in him a haunting sense of the past which his father's words failed to convey. Stephen slips into one of his recurrent reveries about himself—

> He recalled his own equivocal position in Belvedere, a free
> boy, a leader afraid of his own authority, proud and sensi-
> tive and suspicious...

His father's repeated and empty sounding advice always to be a good fellow, a good Catholic, and above all a gentleman, falls on deaf ears.

Stephen endures a further humiliation making the round of local pubs with his father where Simon's old cronies hearken back to tales of Stephen's great grandfather, "a fierce old fireeater." Their camaraderie leaves him unmoved—"Nothing stirred within his soul but a cold and cruel and loveless lust."

The next scene describes Stephen and his family going to the bank to collect the prize money which he has won in an essay contest. Stephen indulges in a splurge of lavish spending on his family. He lifts them briefly from their poverty, takes them to the theater, and buys extravagant presents. But the spree is short-lived and, as life returns to its former pattern, he feels even more strongly his "futile isolation." Even money had not succeeded in bridging the gap between himself and the world he was trying to approach.

Stephen's fierce longings lead him inevitably away from the drab paralyzed world of his home and school. He revels in "secret riots," and is overwhelmed by "savage desires." He walks the streets at night "like a baffled prowling beast" and begins to frequent the squalid quarter of the brothels. As the chapter closes, we witness Stephen's seduction scene. He wanders down a Dublin street and a

26

young woman in a doorway detains him; she invites him to her room, and there he "surrendered himself to her, body and mind..."

Commentary

The events of Chapter II demonstrate clearly Stephen's unhappy relationship with his father. This problem of paternity becomes a major theme in Joyce's work and is generally referred to as the *search for the father motif.* This theme has become almost a twentieth-century preoccupation and is prominent in the work of Thomas Wolfe, William Faulkner, and D. H. Lawrence, to mention only a few. Joyce's heroes invariably suffer because of their relationship to a father figure, whether it be priest, teacher, or actual father. Stephen's psychological search for a father is more fully developed in *Ulysses,* but the theme has its roots in *Portrait of the Artist.*

Simon Dedalus is a continual source of humiliation and disappointment to his son: "Any allusion made to his father by a fellow or by a master put his calm to rout in a moment." Stephen remains to the end, the unforgiving son who views his father as an improvident foster-parent.

Just as in the ancient myth of Daedalus and Icarus, Joyce is interpreting the modern day problem as that of the son against the father for the mastery of the universe. On this symbolic level, the father figure becomes a kind of initiatory priest who should guide the son into the larger adult world. Simon Dedalus, like most of Joyce's fictional fathers, is a glaring failure in this regard. Thus, in reversing the classic pattern, Joyce is able to comment ironically on modern man.

Stephen has developed a silent aloofness in an effort to escape the moral cheapness of his world, and his yearnings for love and beauty lead him into the arms of a whore. But in Stephen's first sexual experience we see that he is still a child and that the woman is really playing a mother role. Joyce's heroes are always both sons and lovers, and his heroines are generally very maternal.

Stephen's moral growth continues along with his delusions of maturity and his social alienation. The "soul's incurable loneliness" was another obsession of Joyce's, and Stephen is the embodiment of that estrangement which constantly measures the distance between souls, and between the ideal and the reality.

CHAPTER III

Summary

Stephen sits in class anticipating a heavy meal and an evening of revelling in the brothel district. As he gazes at the equations written on his paper he indulges in another of his careful self appraisals. He acknowledges all his excesses and the possibility of eternal damnation, and yet repentance was impossible for him even though he senses that a wave of vitality has passed out of him and would return no more. In fact, "he lusted for his own destruction." He stops going to Mass though he continues to lead the prayers to the Blessed Virgin at Sodality meetings on Saturday mornings. Somehow he feels a stronger attraction to this ideal female, the refuge of sinners, and he is soothed by these litanies in her honor.

He sits in catechism class and almost enjoys wrestling with the questions of religious doctrine which the rector poses, even though the discussion magnifies his own sense of sin. With clinical scrutiny he analyzes his downfall—"From the evil seed of lust all other deadly sins had sprung forth." The rector announces the approaching three day retreat to be held in honor of the feast of Saint Francis Xavier, the patron saint of the college. The rector recounts briefly the life of this great saint.

The retreat begins and Stephen sits in the front bench of the chapel as the retreat master embarks on the first of his long discourses concerning the "four last things," namely—death, judgment, hell and heaven. He entreats the boys to compose themselves for three days of meditative silence. As the lectures proceed, Stephen's fears for his soul begin to mount. He thinks about the "particular judgment" upon his death and, worse yet, the "general judgment" at the end of the world when all mankind would be tried before the Supreme Judge. All his secret sins would be made known, and it would be too late to repent. Every word the preacher utters seems aimed directly at him. He thinks about the girl named

Emma who had so often been the subject of his evil thoughts, and the sordid "packet of pictures" he kept and the "foul long letters" he composed and furtively placed where some girl might find them.

Another session begins, and the preacher outlines the fall of Lucifer, the creation of Adam and Eve, their banishment from paradise, and the eventual coming of the Redeemer, Jesus Christ.

But the heart of his discussion is a consideration of the nature of hell, and he accomplishes a meticulous dissection of the torments of that place of the damned. He elaborates on all the pains that each sense is subjected to: the eyes with impenetrable darkness, the nose with a horrid stench, the ears with screeching and howling noises, the taste with foul and decayed matter, and the touch with burning spikes and never-consuming flames. As the speaker warms to his topic he dwells on the attributes of those fiendish devils who spend eternity afflicting the damned souls. Finally he entones a solemn warning: "Time is, time was, but time shall be no more!"

Trembling and terrified, Stephen leaves the chapel and returns to his classroom. He imagines for a moment that he had already died and been plunged into the inferno. But the voices of Vincent Heron and Mr. Tate, his teacher, draw him back to reality, and he realizes that there is still time to be saved. Though he has never felt so humble and contrite, a faint chill sweeps over him at the thought of having to put all his hideous sins into words in confession.

The final lecture of the retreat is devoted to the *spiritual* torments which the damned soul must undergo. First is the *pain of loss.* One knows that he has lost all hope of God and of goodness forever. The second is the *pain of conscience* which is a perpetual feeling of remorse. The third is the *pain of extension,* that is, boundless and limitless suffering; coexistent with this is the *pain of intensity.* Since the damned soul is at the centermost point of all evil, suffering achieves the highest degree of intensity, beyond human comprehension. But the ultimate torture of hell, according to the preacher, is the eternity of it all. He uses the classic example of the huge mountain of sand and the little bird carrying away a grain every million years. Even after he has carried away a square foot of that sand mountain, not one instant of eternity would have passed.

His concluding remarks deal with the awful enormity of a single grievous sin in the eyes of a just God, and he ends the retreat, leading the congregation in an act of contrition.

Thoroughly shaken, Stephen goes to his room and with an aching heart tries to examine his conscience. But exhaustion overtakes him, and he drops off into a dream, a horrible vision of his own personal hell—a reeking swampy field peopled with goatish half human creatures. He awakens with a jerk and becomes sick to his stomach.

That evening he walks to a remote end of town, and a kindly old priest hears his confession. Filled with joy and relief he receives Holy Communion at Mass the following morning and resolves to begin a new life of sanctity.

Commentary

The priest's sermon on hell serves as a moral center to the novel, and it makes Stephen's rejection of his religion in Chapter Five all the more dramatic. It serves the same thematic purpose as Father Mapple's sermon on Jonah in *Moby Dick* or Ivan's legend of the Grand Inquisitor in *The Brothers Karamazov*.[2]

The question of eternal punishment was of great theological interest in the latter part of the nineteenth century. There were numerous tracts and sermons on the subject printed at this time and Joyce, no doubt, had access to the accounts of various religious writers.

But Joyce had an extraordinary memory, and he was able to draw from his own first hand recollections of similar retreats he had attended as a boy. And, although his account has been criticized for being a rather incomplete and one-sided picture of such a retreat, it is still an astonishingly accurate reflection of nineteenth-century Irish Catholic thought on the subject.

We should be aware that Joyce intended a certain amount of humor in the "fire and brimstone" ranting of the preacher and

[2]Harry Levin, *James Joyce* (Norfolk, Conn.: 1960), p. 57.

Stephen's heart-rending remorse. Joyce viewed Stephen with sympathy but also with a detachment that allowed him to find some humor in the young adolescent's soul-struggles.

On the symbolic and mythic level, this three day retreat could be viewed as Stephen's trip to a mythic underworld. The journey of the mythic hero generally includes a physical or mental crisis in which he experiences the torments of hell. This ancient pattern is as old as the Bible and as universal as eastern and western mythology. Such a descent journey is in the tradition of Jonah's entry into the belly of the whale, of Joseph in the well, and the three day entombment of Christ.

Stephen's retreat (journey to hell) lasts three days during which he is led verbally by the priest through the torments of hell. And, like the hero of myth, Stephen comes back from his journey with a boon or elixir. In his case, it is an expansion of consciousness and a change of heart.

Joyce's writing operates on several levels of meaning. By planting clues in his imagery, symbolic and mythic elements work together and are implied simultaneously.

CHAPTER IV

Summary

Stephen begins a fervent round of sacraments and mortification —daily Mass, prayers for the dead, and continual recitation of the rosary he carries in his pocket. "Each of the senses was brought under a rigorous discipline" by little acts of self-denial.

At last he believed in the reality of love, for God had manifested it so directly to him by forgiveness and the grace that had poured into his soul.

And yet, despite his efforts, doubts and scruples began to take root, and he experiences long periods of spiritual dryness. Human frailty, his own and others, left him with a sense of futility and desolation. At the same time he is beset with violent and frequent temptations to sin, and the thought that by one willful act he could wipe out all his spiritual gains, filled him with feelings of power.

Impressed by Stephen's exterior piety and studious habits, the director of the college calls him to his office for an interview. He asks Stephen if he has considered a vocation to the priesthood, and Stephen momentarily imagines himself in this role. He is thrilled by the thought of such secret power and knowledge but "the chill and order of the life repelled him" and he ultimately rejects this way of life.

Disillusioned by his failure to perfect himself, he acknowledges that he will fall from his state of grace. It was inevitable; not to fall was too difficult. He feels remorse towards his brothers and sisters, for he knows that the family has sacrificed everything for his education. Just a step ahead of the bill collectors, the Dedalus family moves again, but his father is determined to get his son into the university.

As the chapter draws to a close, we follow Stephen on one of his frequent walks, this time along the seashore. A group of his friends, enjoying a swim, call out his name, and Stephen is reminded of his mythical prototype Daedalus, "the fabulous artificer." He imagines himself soaring in the sky like that ancient "hawklike man," and he begins to tremble with excitement. He feels that his soul has received a call to life, that he is rising from the grave of his boyhood. As he walks into the water, the reader realizes that Stephen's journey of self-discovery is reaching a climax. He gazes intently at a girl who stands before him in the water, and he feels "a new wild life" in his veins. He stretches out on the sand of the beach to quiet the beating of his heart and he goes to sleep. When he awakens, evening has come.

Commentary

Stephen is identified with both Icarus and Daedalus as the *mythic motif* weaves in and out of the imagery. At times he is like the crafty inventor, Daedalus, imprisoned in the labyrinth (Dublin) but devising a plan of escape. At other times he is like the rebellious and impetuous son, Icarus. Stephen predicts his fall, a fall symbolic of that of Icarus: "He would fall...he would fall silently, in an instant."

At the end of the chapter, during Stephen's epiphany, he becomes convinced that his name, Dedalus, is a prophecy of the end he is to serve—a symbol of the artist and a call to life. He will create, with the power and freedom of that great artificer, Daedalus.

Stephen's quest for a father continues. For Joyce, the individual and national search for the father are rooted in the same psychological soil. When Stephen speaks of the "disorder, the misrule and confusion of his father's house...." he is referring not only to Simon Dedalus but also to Ireland itself. Joyce consciously cut himself away from nationalist movements and social crusades out of a sense of futility and disillusionment.

The climax of the book occurs as Stephen walks along the seashore. His moment of spiritual revelation or epiphany is signaled by the sight of a lovely girl standing in the water. She is a symbol of futurity for Stephen, and her presence announces an impending spiritual rebirth for him. The baptismal quality of the experience is emphasized by the water imagery.

Now Stephen sees himself clearly for the first time. He knows what he must do with his life. He has been called to another kind of priesthood, that of the artist. For Stephen, the life of the church would have meant order but a denial of the senses, a renunciation of life. Instead, he will seek an affirmation of life in the power of words to confer an order and life of their own.

Joyce's writing during the epiphany section is closer to incantation than description. He is working with the sound and rhythm of words, and as he spins his sentences the meanings of the words slip into the background. Their meaning is not particularly important to his aesthetic purpose. Stephen, voicing Joyce's own position, remarks that he is not sure whether he loves "the rhythmic rise and fall of words better than their association of legend and colour."

Such a sentence as, "A world, a glimmer, or a flower? Glimmering and trembling and unfolding, a breaking light, an opening flower, it spread in endless succession to itself..." is virtually meaningless if logically analyzed and seems closer to poetry than prose.

CHAPTER V

Summary

Stephen is now enrolled at the university. It is morning, and Stephen is late for class. His father shouts at him for his laziness. His mother concurs that university life has changed him.

The young intellectual has emerged full-blown, absorbed in the search for beauty and the essence of art. Cranly, a fellow student, shares his esoteric interests. Stephen becomes a kind of disciple before the priest-like figure of Cranly and confides in him all the secret longings of his heart.

His university companions are mentioned throughout the chapter, and various encounters are described. Davin is one companion. An ardent Irish nationalist, Stephen considers him a "dull-witted loyal serf." But Stephen, ever fascinated with language and the sound of words, is intrigued by Davin's speech — an interesting mixture of Elizabethan English and quaint Irish idioms. Davin's description of an incident after a hurling match provides Joyce with an opportunity to demonstrate his proficiency in imitating the Irish vernacular speech.

The incident involves a lonely walk home late one night during which Davin stops at an isolated cottage to ask for a mug of milk. The peasant woman who answers the door terrifies the young student by her mysterious manner and her urgent requests that he come in and spend the night with her. He leaves quickly but never forgets the encounter.

Having interrupted the time sequence of the action, Joyce returns to the morning described at the beginning of the chapter when Stephen was setting off for class. Upon arrival Stephen goes to the physics theater (lecture hall) and meets the Dean of Studies who is lighting a fire in the hearth. A discussion follows in which they talk about the useful arts (lighting a fire) versus the liberal arts which in turn leads to a theoretical discourse on the object of the artist. Stephen says that the object of the artist must be the creation of the beautiful, and the Dean asks Stephen what he considers the beautiful. Quoting from his favorite source, St. Thomas Aquinas, Stephen states that "those things are beautiful the perception of which pleases."

Stephen attempts to formulate his own aesthetic philosophy, and he uses various persons (the Dean, Cranly, and Lynch) to test his ideas. He tells the Dean that he uses the ideas of Aquinas as a lamp to light his own thinking. There can be no such thing as free thinking, he maintains, for all thinking must be bound by its own laws.

Stephen's discussion with the Dean ends as the physics professor and the other students enter the hall, and class begins. As the professor lectures, Stephen watches in a condescending manner as his fellow students carry on their wisecracking horse-play.

After class Stephen meets Cranly. A group of students are busy enlisting students to sign a petition for disarmament and world peace. Stephen says that the matter is of no interest to him. Temple, one of the more emotional members of the group, walks off with Stephen and Cranly, firing questions at Stephen whose knowledge obviously impresses him.

Davin and another student named Lynch join Stephen and Cranly as they watch a hurling match. Stephen denounces Davin's blind patriotism, saying that he does not share the other's strong allegiance to his country; "Ireland is an old sow that eats her farrow," he concludes coldly.

Lynch and Stephen break away from the others, and Stephen begins to hold forth on his aesthetic philosophy. His philosophy, which he refers to as "applied Aquinas," follows.

1547673
STEPHEN'S AESTHETIC THEORY

Two chief principles (from Thomas Aquinas):

1. Those things are beautiful the perception of which pleases.

2. The good is that toward which the appetite tends.

    a. The creative artist is concerned only with the creation of the beautiful.

    b. The productive artist is concerned with the production of the good.

3. Art must produce a *stasis* in the observer; that is, it seeks no end but the satisfaction of an aesthetic sense.

4. Art should not be *kinetic;* that is, it should not produce an emotion such as desire or loathing. If it does it assumes the function of a useful art, such as rhetoric.

5. Three things are necessary for the perception of the beautiful:

    a. wholeness or integrity

    b. harmony or proportion

    c. clarity or radiance

Using the example of a basket, Stephen elaborates on the three things necessary for the perception of the beautiful. First, one sees the basket as *one* thing (wholeness); then one perceives it as *a* thing with parts (harmony); finally one sees it as *that* thing and *no other* thing (clarity). Stephen explains to Lynch that beauty and truth produce a *stasis* in the mind of the observer. He quotes Plato: "Beauty is the splendor of the truth."

As they proceed on their walk, Stephen divides art into a progression of three forms:

1. *The lyrical:* the image is presented in immediate relation to the artist himself.

2. *The epic:* the image is presented in immediate relation to the artist and to others (not purely personal).

3. *The dramatic:* the image is presented in immediate relation to others. The artist's personality is refined out of existence (impersonal).

It begins to rain, and Lynch and Stephen return to the library. Lynch points out Stephen's girl as she walks off with her companions. Stephen watches her closely without calling to her and is oblivious of his friend's conversation.

The next scene finds Stephen lying in bed early one morning with pencil and paper composing stanzas of verse for a villanelle. The girl who is so frequently mentioned in Stephen's thoughts is the subject of the poem. He calls to mind the many times thay have been together over the past ten years — that many years have passed since the tram ride together (see Chapter II). He finally writes out the six stanzas of the completed villanelle.

Another abrupt change of locale, and Stephen is standing on the steps of the library watching the birds circling above his head. It reminds him again of the flight of Daedalus. Stephen resolves that he must leave not only his home but his church and his country.

A group of bantering students form again on the library steps — Dixon, Temple, Glynn, Cranly, and Stephen. Stephen sees the girl again and follows her for a short distance as his companions dispute where unbaptized infants go upon their death.

Stephen asks Cranly to step away from the group, and he explains that he has had an argument about religion with his mother. She had asked him to make his Easter duty, that is, to go to Mass and communion. Stephen refuses to do this and repeats to Cranly the *non serviam* of Lucifer: "I will not serve." The controlled and analytical Cranly points out the irony of Stephen's mental saturation with a religion in which he no longer believes. They discuss Stephen's parents. He loves his mother, but he considers his father merely "a praiser of his own past."

Cranly tells Stephen he should grant his mother her request since Stephen apparently does not take the religious ritual seriously. Stephen retorts that he neither believes nor disbelieves, but admits that he is not sure enough of his disbelief to risk making a sacrilegious communion. Stephen respects the forms and rituals of the Church by refusing to observe them. In answer to Cranly, he states that he does not intend to become a Protestant, forsaking a logical and coherent absurdity for an illogical and incoherent one. He believes that he must go away in order to have unfettered spiritual freedom.

In a strong statement of his intention, he declares that he cannot serve that in which he no longer believes whether it be Church, home, or fatherland. He will live as best he can, defending himself with the only arms he allows himself — silence, exile, and cunning. Furthermore, he does not fear to be alone or forsaken or to make a mistake — even a mistake as long as eternity.

The last section of the book is a series of dated entries in Stephen's diary as he prepares to leave Ireland. The first one is dated March 20th, and his last entry is made on April 27th. Stephen describes his final meetings with Lynch, Cranly, and Davin, and writes down his thoughts and impressions in brief, journalistic phrases. He tells his mother that he cannot return to the Church; he cannot repent.

He describes his last meeting with his girl friend at which both are nervous and remote. Stephen feigns a self-assured detachment. He turns on "his spiritual-heroic refrigerating apparatus, invented and patented in all countries by Dante Alighieri" thereby associating his protracted romance with the unrealized, ideal love of Dante and Beatrice.

The last entry of the novel in which he calls out to his ancient mythic father, Daedalus, is by now a classic of English prose:

April 26…So be it. Welcome, O Life! I go to encounter for the millionth time the reality of experience and to forge in the smithy of my soul the uncreated conscience of my race. April 27. Old father, old artificer, stand me now and ever in good stead.

Commentary

This final chapter which is the longest and most dense section of the book, chronicles Stephen's rebellion. In the course of nearly eighty pages of prose nothing really *happens* to Stephen in the sense of a dramatic event occurring. The only "action" which takes place is the seemingly endless walks which Stephen takes around the campus of the university, during which he expounds his thoughts and theories to his companions. But he is making progress on his journey of self-discovery.

One by one, Stephen knocks down those blocks to his future progress—family, church, and country. Through his conversation with Davin we observe Stephen's utter disinterest in the social and political problems of his country. Davin's ardent nationalism bores him. In this connection, it is interesting and a bit ironic that Joyce should spend the remainder of his life, nearly forty years, writing exclusively about the country and the people which he rejected so completely at the age of twenty.

In his conversations with Cranly, Stephen explains why he must disregard the dictates of his church and his family in order to achieve his purpose in life. The idealistic Stephen, seeking spiritual perfection in himself and in his religion, finds only organized materialism and superficial piety in the Church.

On the positive side, while he is verbally tearing down the old order, Stephen is building up his own personal philosophy of life and an elaborate aesthetic theory. These are revealed by means of conversations with the dean of studies and another classmate, Lynch.

The style of writing in this chapter is, for the most part, discursive; that is, Stephen's arguments proceed from premises to conclusions in a series of logical steps. The style is discursive also in the sense that Joyce covers a formidable amount of ground by continually rambling and digressing from one subject to another.

The *search for the father motif* is sounded again in the person of Cranly, Stephen's classmate and confidant. Stephen's description of Cranly in "priest-like" terms points up the awe and respect with which he views Cranly. He becomes another kind of substitute father for the searching Stephen, and he comes closest to answering this psychological need in Stephen: "...he had told Cranly of all the tumults and unrest and longings in his soul, day after day and night by night, only to be answered by his friend's listening silence...."

Stephen's discussion with the Dean of Studies is interesting not only for the theories of art that are expounded but also for the fire and light metaphor which is developed. We recall from Chapter II that Stephen's great grandfather was referred to as a "fierce old fireeater." This image is played off Stephen's remark to the dean of studies: "I am sure I could not light a fire." Furthermore, Stephen explains that he uses the ideas of Thomas Aquinas as a lamp to light his way into the depths of philosophy. Such references to light and fire work with the imagery of blindness that runs through the novel. Weak vision, both spiritual and physical, is a recurrent theme in *Portrait of the Artist*.

The Dean of Studies voices a fatherly warning to Stephen in regard to his pursuit of knowledge: "Many go down to the depths and never come up." His cautioning tone and the water metaphor suggest the mythic relationship of the father Daedalus to the impetuous novice, Icarus.

Stephen identifies with the Daedalus myth directly as he stands on the library steps gazing at the birds' flight above him. It reminds him of "the hawklike man whose name he bore soaring out of his captivity...." Stephen resolves to soar out of his captivity also.

In this final chapter, critics generally agree that Joyce was preparing the character of Stephen Dedalus for *Ulysses* in which he plays a principal role. Some feel that the rather humorless, pedantic turn that Stephen's personality takes in this last chapter makes him not an artist at all but merely an esthete. Others believe that Stephen's entries in his journal indicate the beginnings of wisdom. At any rate, we leave Stephen in a somewhat unfinished state, ready to be polished off by Joyce in *Ulysses*.

In the end Stephen sets out to discover "what the heart is and what feels." He is still lonely and fearful and immature, but at least he is aware of some of the problems and perhaps better capable of controlling them.

A REVIEW OF THEMES AND MOTIFS

A motif is a repeated word, idea, or image which acts as a unifying device and is a way of presenting theme at any given moment without stating it. A word or image, such as fire, blind, or light in *Portrait of the Artist*, crosses and recrosses the fabric of the story and creates a kind of internal stitching. Motifs bind a novel together and are often the one cohesive element in many sprawling works of art.

Portrait of the Artist is shot through with symbolism and, no doubt, several thematic motifs could be discovered by the perceptive reader. Joyce's use of symbolic motifs is often subtle and develops like ripples on water, expanding in many directions. Good symbols refuse to be hard and specific in order to suggest larger possibilities of meaning.

We have suggested thematic motifs and given them names, but this in no way is intended to limit other possible motifs and other interpretations of them. The beauty of Joyce's writing is its inexhaustible richness.

THE BLINDNESS MOTIF

The blindness motif includes all the images of light and darkness, of sight and lack of vision. The motif begins in the first pages of the story. Stephen recalls a childhood verse he learned from his

Aunt Dante: "Pull out his eyes / Apologize..." This is a fearful image to the young boy, and he continues to be concerned about his weak vision throughout his childhood. The incident on the playing field when his glasses are knocked off and broken leads to the humiliating punishment he receives from Father Dolan in Latin class at Clongowes. Stephen says of himself: "He felt his body small and weak...and his eyes were weak and watery." He has a child's terror of darkness: "O, the road there between the trees was dark! You would be lost in the dark. It made him afraid to think of how it was." And even at the age of twenty Stephen includes in the small list of things that he fears, "country roads at night." The reader will notice how frequently the descriptive words "dark," "firey," or "flaming," are repeated. Stephen's great-grandfather is called a "fierce old fireeater."

This fire and light aspect of the blindness motif becomes very obvious in Chapter V during Stephen's philosophical discussion with the Dean of Studies. They begin by discussing the art of lighting a fire as the dean is attempting to start a fire in the hearth. Then, pursuing the same metaphor, Stephen tells the dean that he uses the ideas of certain philosophers as lamps to light the way of his own thinking. Pointing up his own sense of inadequacy, Stephen says to the dean: "I am sure I could not light a fire."

This blindness motif serves to emphasize the plight of the young boy who is searching not only for answers to philosophical questions but also for *insight* into the adult world he sees around him but cannot understand.

As an adolescent, Stephen is not only physically afflicted with weak eyesight, but he is also "blinded" by romantic illusions. This is especially evident in his unrealistic attitude toward various ideal females, for example, the fictional Mercedes of *The Count of Monte Cristo*. As a child he has only partial vision of his world, but by the end of the novel he has lost at least some of his illusions and is able to "see" the meaning of his life more clearly.

THE MYTHIC MOTIF

The mythic motif is introduced through the name of the hero, Stephen Dedalus. Joyce used the ancient Greek myth of Daedalus and Icarus (see section entitled The Use of Myth) as a background story from which to compare and contrast his modern story of Stephen Dedalus.

As a child at Clongowes in Chapter I, Stephen is questioned by his classmate, Nasty Roche: "What kind of name is that?" And although he is unable to grasp the meaning of such a remark he begins to sense that his unusual last name may be the portent of some future destiny. Later in the novel Stephen identifies himself directly with his mythic prototypes. Sometimes he identifies with the crafty inventor Daedalus who devised an escape from the labyrinth. At other times he resembles closely in his attitudes the rebellious ill-fated son Icarus who flies too high and is plunged to his death in the sea.

All the images of flight and of water work in with this motif. For Stephen, Dublin is a modern labyrinth, a place of confinement from which he must escape. In Chapter V as he stands on the steps of the university library he gazes at the birds' flight above him, and he is reminded of that "hawklike man whose name he bore soaring out of his captivity...." Stephen believes that he must leave Ireland in order to be free.

At the climax of the book which occurs at the end of Chapter IV the mythic motif is strongly evident. Stephen is standing in the water and practically all the imagery deals with birds and flight. Even the unknown girl he is watching seems to be "changed into the likeness of a strange and beautiful seabird." Now at this moment of his epiphany (see section on The Epiphany) he sensed that his "strange name" was a prophecy:

> he seemed to hear the noise of dim waves and to see a winged form flying above the waves and slowly climbing the air. What did it mean? Was it...a hawklike man flying sunward above the sea, a prophecy of the end he had been born to serve...a symbol of the artist....

Thus, through the use of symbolic imagery, Joyce compares the ancient flight of Daedalus and Icarus with the modern day flight of Stephen Dedalus away from his captivity in Dublin.

THE SEARCH FOR THE FATHER MOTIF

This theme or motif is a popular one in twentieth-century literature. We see it in the works of Thomas Wolfe, William Faulkner, and D. H. Lawrence. This problem of paternity is a major theme in all of Joyce's writing. His heroes, especially Stephen Dedalus, invariably suffer because of their relationship to a father figure, whether it be priest, teacher, or actual father. Simon Dedalus, Stephen's father, is a continual source of humiliation to his son: "Any allusion made to his father by a fellow or by a master put his calm to rout in a moment." And Stephen remains to the end, the unforgiving son who views his father, Simon, as an improvident foster-parent, "a praiser of his own past."

The failure of Simon Dedalus to measure up to his son's expectations causes Stephen to set out on a psychological search for a father which continues in Joyce's later book, *Ulysses*. Many of the priests and teachers in *Portrait of the Artist* become father figures for the searching Stephen. During Stephen's philosophical discussion with the Dean of Studies in Chapter V, the Dean sounds a fatherly warning to Stephen which reminds one of the fatherly warning Daedalus gave to his son Icarus before their flight over the sea:

It is like looking down from the cliffs of Moher into the depths. Many go down into the depths and never come up. Only the trained diver can go down into those depths and explore them and come to the surface again.

Like the impetuous Icarus, Stephen is eager to explore strange new worlds, and it is the wise father who should guide the young fledgling into the more complex adult world. Stephen's real father, Simon, is a monumental failure in this regard, at least from Stephen's point of view. And the substitute fathers that Stephen seeks are often ineffectual in their actions and dogmatic in their thinking.

Cranly, Stephen's classmate, comes closest perhaps in answering this psychological need in the young artist: "...he had told Cranly of all the tumults and unrest and longings in his soul, day after day and night by night, only to be answered by his friend's listening silence...." Cranly's persistent questioning of Stephen in regard to his religion and his refusal to obey his mother's requests upsets Stephen and disturbs his single-minded intention to break all his ties with the past. But in the end Stephen severs all these relationships and sets out on his journey, still spiritually fatherless, still searching. In the final sentence of the novel Stephen calls out to his ancient mythic father, Daedalus: "Old father, old artificer, stand me now and ever in good stead."

GLOSSARY OF PERSONS, PLACES, AND TERMS

Aristotle
Third century B.C., Greek philosopher. Stephen Dedalus derives many of the ideas for his own aesthetic philosophy from Aristotle.

Art
Stephen Dedalus defines art as "the human disposition of sensible or intelligible matter for an esthetic end."

Capuchin
A Franciscan order of monks. A capuchin monk hears Stephen's confession at the age of sixteen.

Cardinal Newman (John Henry)
Nineteenth-century English theologian and writer. Stephen considers him the greatest prose writer.

castle, the
The building at Clongowes Wood College which houses the community of Jesuit priests. The rector's office which Stephen visits is in the castle.

catechism
A handbook of questions and answers used to teach the fundamentals of religion.

Charles Stewart Parnell (1846-1891)

The Irish statesman who is the subject of the political argument which breaks up a Christmas dinner in the Dedalus home. As leader of the Irish Nationalist Party he fought to secure home rule for Ireland. In 1890 a Captain O'Shea sued his wife, Kitty, for divorce naming Parnell corespondent in the suit. This scandal split the party into two factions and brought about Parnell's political ruin. He was denounced by some people as an adulterer although he eventually married Kitty O'Shea.

Confiteor

A Latin word meaning "I confess"; it is a formal prayer recited during a Roman Catholic Mass. In Chapter II Stephen recites this prayer to his companions in mock seriousness.

Cork

One of the larger cities on the southern coast of Ireland. Stephen accompanies his father on a trip to this city where they visit Simon Dedalus' *alma mater,* Queens College.

Count of Monte Cristo, The

Stephen's favorite adventure story as a young boy (see Chapter II). It is a nineteenth-century novel by the elder Alexandre Dumas in which the hero, Edmund Dantes, is unjustly imprisoned in a chateau. His situation looks hopeless until he devises a daring escape by feigning death and allowing himself to be lowered into the sea.

Eucharist

The consecrated bread and wine used in the Holy Communion service.

hurling match

An Irish game similar to field hockey.

Jesuit

A member of the Society of Jesus, a Roman Catholic religious order founded by Ignatius Loyola in 1534 (abbreviated S. J.). Stephen's entire formal education was in Jesuit schools in Ireland.

kinesis

To move, of or resulting from motion. According to Stephen's aesthetic theories, art should not be kinetic; that is, it should not produce an emotion such as desire or loathing in the beholder. See also *stasis*.

Limbo

A belief held by some Christian theologies that there exists an abode after death for unbaptized children and righteous people who lived before Jesus. This question is disputed by Stephen and his classmates in Chapter V.

Lord Byron

Nineteenth-century English Romantic poet. An aristocratic rebel, he became the hero of his own poems. Stephen considers Byron the greatest poet.

Lord Tennyson

Nineteenth-century poet of Victorian England. In Stephen's hierarchy of literary giants, he dismisses Tennyson as a mere "rhymster."

Michael Davitt

Nineteenth-century Irish journalist and founder of the Irish Land League. He worked closely with Parnell to further the cause of Irish independence and spent ten years in prison for his efforts. Stephen recalls that Aunt Dante had a hairbrush with a maroon velvet back in honor of Davitt.

motif

A recurring word, image, or idea which acts as a unifying device and often serves to point up the theme or controlling ideas of the novel.

pandybat

An instrument used to strike the palms of the hands as punishment. Stephen was "pandied" by Father Dolan at Clongowes.

pity
Stephen's definition as part of his aesthetic theories: "The feeling which arrests the mind in the presence of whatsoever is grave and constant in human suffering and unites it with the human sufferer." See also "terror."

prefect
Any of various administrative officials. As head of the school sodality, Stephen is called a prefect. Father Dolan at Clongowes is called the prefect of studies.

Queens College
The school in Cork, Ireland, attended by Stephen's father, Simon Dedalus. Stephen and his father pay a visit to the school in Chapter II.

retreat
A period of time in which one withdraws from his everyday affairs for religious contemplation. Stephen makes a three day retreat at Belvedere College which is recounted in Chapter III.

rhythm
Stephen's definition: "The first formal esthetic relation of part to part in any esthetic whole or of an esthetic whole to its part or parts or of any part to the esthetic whole of which it is a part."

Saint Francis Xavier
Sixteenth-century Spanish Jesuit missionary who was called "the Apostle of the Indies." The three day retreat Stephen attends at Belvedere is held in honor of this saint who is the patron saint of the school.

Saint Ignatius of Loyola
Sixteenth-century Spanish founder of the Society of Jesus, an order of priests called Jesuits.

Saint Thomas Aquinas
Thirteenth-century Dominican monk and theologian. Noted for his logical and persuasive argumentation, his philosophical system

is one of the most important products of the Middle Ages. In constructing his own aesthetic philosophy, Stephen draws heavily from Aristotle and Aquinas. In fact, Stephen's theories are referred to as "applied Aquinas."

Sodality of the Blessed Virgin Mary

A religious association formed to carry on devotional and charitable work. Stephen Dedalus is prefect (head) of this organization at Belvedere. They meet on Saturday mornings and recite prayers in honor of the Blessed Virgin.

stasis

According to Stephen's aesthetic theories, art must produce a *stasis* in the observer; that is, art should seek no end but the satisfaction of an aesthetic sense. *Stasis* is the opposite of *kinesis;* it is a static emotion which does not seek to move the observer.

terror

Stephen's definition: "The feeling which arrests the mind in the presence of whatever is grave and constant in human sufferings and unites it with the secret cause."

villanelle

A short poem consisting of three-line stanzas except for the last stanza which has four lines. Stephen composes a villanelle to "E— —C— —" in Chapter V.

Whitsuntide Play

The custom at Belvedere College of holding an annual play during the week of Whitsunday (Pentecost). Stephen plays the role of a farcical pedagogue in the Whitsuntide play described in Chapter II.

Wolf Tone

Eighteenth-century Irish revolutionist who formed a society to combat English Protestant "oppressors." As a soldier of fortune he had dealings with the French and was eventually sentenced to death as a traitor. He committed suicide in a Dublin prison in 1798.

QUESTIONS FOR REVIEW

Note: The chapter or section indicated in parentheses after each question contains information which will help to answer the question.

1. Is this novel an autobiography in the strict sense of the term? Discuss the relationship between the author and Stephen Dedalus. (Section II. Is STEPHEN DEDALUS JAMES JOYCE? and Section III. LIFE AND BACKGROUND)

2. Joyce's writing is noted for auditory rather than visual images. Discuss. (Section IV. STYLE AND LITERARY TECHNIQUES)

3. What is the stream-of-consciousness technique? Illustrate its use by referring to passages in the novel. (Section IV – A: Stream-of-Consciousness)

4. Describe what an "epiphany" is in Joyce's writing. Where does the major epiphany occur in this novel? (Section IV – B: Epiphany)

5. What purposes does the use of myth serve in *Portrait of the Artist?* (Section IV – C: Use of Myth)

6. Discuss the relationship between the myth of Daedalus and Icarus and the character of Stephen Dedalus? (Section IV – C: Use of Myth and Section VIII. The Mythic Motif)

7. What are motifs in literature? What purpose do they serve in this novel? (Chapter I Commentary: Section VIII. RE-VIEW OF THEMES AND MOTIFS)

8. Explain the significance of the *search for the father motif* in this novel. (See Commentaries for Chapters II and V; Section VIII. The Search for the Father Motif)

9. Why did the author devote almost an entire chapter to a sermon on hell? (Chapter III: Commentary)

10. Where does the turning point or climax of the novel occur, and how is Stephen changed by this experience? (Chapter IV: Summary and Commentary)

NOTES

NOTES

NOTES

NOTES

NOTES

NOTES